Danger!
Children at Work

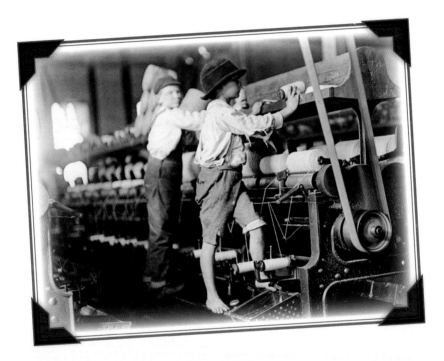

by Sharon Franklin

Editorial Offices: Glenview, Illinois • Parsippany, New Jersey • New York, New York
Sales Offices: Needham, Massachusetts • Duluth, Georgia • Glenview, Illinois
Coppell, Texas • Ontario, California • Mesa, Arizona

Photographs

Every effort has been made to secure permission and provide appropriate credit for photographic material. The publisher deeply regrets any omission and pledges to correct errors called to its attention in subsequent editions.

Unless otherwise acknowledged, all photographs are the property of Pearson Education.

Photo locators denoted as follows: Top (T), Center (C), Bottom (B), Left (L), Right (R), Background (Bkgd)

Cover: ©Everett Collection Inc/Alamy; **1** ©Everett Collection Inc/Alamy; **3** ©Brand X Pictures; **4** ©PhotoAlto; **5** ©Library of Congress; **7** (T, B) ©The Protected Art Archive/Alamy; **8** ©Library of Congress; **9** ©Library of Congress; **11** (T) ©Library of Congress, (B) ©Everett Collection Inc/Alamy; **12** ©Everett Collection Inc/Alamy; **13** ©Library of Congress; **15** ©Library of Congress; **16** ©Library of Congress; **17** ©Courtesy: CSU Archives/Everett Collection Inc/Alamy; **19** (T) ©Library of Congress, (B) ©National Archives; **20** ©David King/DK Images; **21** ©Brand X Pictures; **22** (TL) ©Library of Congress; (TR) ©1984 Harry N. Abrams, Inc., NY. Photo by Lewis Hine/National Archives, (BL) ©Everett Collection Inc/Alamy; (BR) ©Brand X Pictures

ISBN: 0-328-13438-4

16 17 18 19 V0FL 16 15 14 13

What responsibilities do you have at home? Maybe you have to feed the dog and clean your room. Perhaps you have to do the dishes or take out the trash. Do you think it is unfair, having to do so much work?

Believe it or not, the chores you and other young people do today are nothing compared to the hard, dangerous work many children did less than one hundred years ago! Picture this.

What kinds of chores do you do?

It is dark outside, as you would expect it to be at 3 A.M., when most people are sleeping. But Nellie, a thin, scraggly-haired seven-year-old with sad green eyes, is waiting at the dock, as she has done nightly for nearly a year. She is waiting for the oyster boats to unload their cargo. Near the dock, in the dim light, is a huge pile of oyster shells. Soon Nellie hurries off to take her place shucking oysters. Later in the day, she will start peeling shrimp.

Nellie uses her small hands and a sharp knife to pry open the oyster shells and drop the meat into a pail. When Nellie's pail is full, she carries it off to be weighed. Nellie usually fills one or two pails each day.

The oyster shells are sharp on little fingers, but the shrimp are even worse. When peeled, they ooze acid that eats holes in shoes and even in Nellie's tin pail. Many children, including Nellie, have swollen, bleeding fingers. Nellie, and many other children like her, stand up to do this job for ten to twelve hours, sometimes working until midnight. They do not get a short break until late afternoon. They earn less than fifty cents a day.

Shucking oysters is tough work on little fingers.

The Start of Child Labor

Since ancient times, many children have worked with their families to do their part as a family member. The practice of **child labor,** however, is different. Child labor uses and often misuses children in a workplace that benefits only employers. It started in Europe in the 1700s with the production of iron and the use of coal to power machines. The new industrial societies used child labor.

Society was changing in the United States as well. Many factories were being built there in the 1800s. Children were often forced to work alongside their parents in the factories or mines to make ends meet.

Factories filled with big machines churned out products that were once made by hand by skilled workers in small workshops. To the workers' **dismay,** the factories did not need their skills anymore. Unskilled workers could tend the machines and perform the repetitive, boring work for much less money.

Children were highly desirable as a source of unskilled labor. They kept production costs down because they worked for lower pay than adults. They did not question authority, and employers thought they were not likely to cause problems.

Children and their mothers work cutting string beans.

Children and their mothers work shucking oysters.

Large numbers of poor people immigrated to the United States during the time when factories needed unskilled labor. Immigrants came from Germany, Italy, Ireland, and other countries. Between 1901 and 1910 more than eight million people came to live in the United States. Many of these new immigrants had little education and desperately needed money.

Many immigrant children were sent off to work at a young age. They were willing to work hard for money just to survive. In some places, for adults to get jobs, they had to have children who could work. Others lied about their children's ages in order to get them on the factory **payroll.**

These people are Italian immigrants at Ellis Island.

Wanted: Child Workers

In the early 1900s not all children went to work. Children from wealthy families did not need to earn money. They played outside, went swimming, ate healthy meals, enjoyed ice cream during the summer, and snuggled next to warm coal fires in the winter.

Their lives were very different from the lives of the poor children working on the street. These young laborers sold newspapers to the fortunate children's parents. They dug the coal that warmed their houses or made the fabric for their clothes. Poor children often worked ten to twelve hours a day, six days a week. They worked in cramped, dimly lit factories, in the darkness of the mines, or in the freezing cold or blistering hot sun outside. Children often worked in dangerous, unhealthy environments to earn a week's wages that might only buy their family a loaf of bread. They could not attend school because they were always working.

These boys, called newsies, are ready to sell newspapers.

Many children worked for businesses called **sweatshops.** In sweatshops boys and girls worked long hours under dangerous and dirty conditions for low wages. Children working in fabric-making **textile mills** often experienced the worst sweatshop conditions.

The textile process begins with the making of cotton, wool, or silk thread. It ends with fabric that is made from the thread. In cotton mills many girls as young as five years old were hired as **spinners.** Boys younger than seven were hired as **doffers.**

The spinners brushed lint off of the machines. They watched the **bobbins,** as they filled with thread, for any breaks in the thread. When they spotted a break, they had to fix it quickly by tying the ends of the thread together. Spinners usually worked eleven or twelve hours a day, six days a week, and were on their feet nearly all that time.

Doffers removed the full bobbins and replaced them with empty bobbins. Most doffers worked barefoot so they could climb onto the machines. Some slipped, losing fingers and toes in the process. Others fell to their deaths if they slipped into the moving machines.

Spinners (above) and doffers (below) tend their machines.

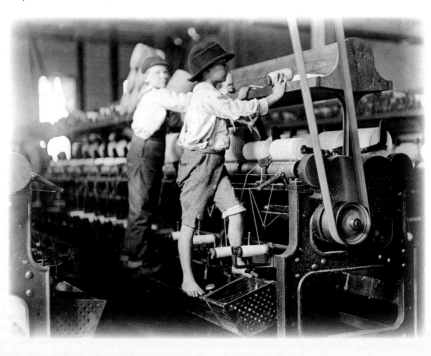

Children help make artificial flowers.

Other businesses paid families to do finish work from their homes in **tenement houses.** These buildings were small, overcrowded, dirty apartments where poor immigrant families lived. Some families worked ten to twelve hours a day in miserable conditions doing piecework such as sewing buttons on coats. This was a good system for employers because they could pay these workers very little for valuable work.

Some families worked making artificial flowers. A family who made 2,000 roses in one day might earn $1.20. Even three-year-old children were put to work making forget-me-not flowers. The small children could make 540 flowers a day. They were paid five cents.

No matter how bad the weather, newsies, or young newspaper sellers—some as young as five years old—got up at five in the morning and worked until after midnight. Many of these children died. Some delivery boys froze to death in their wagons. Many children grew sick from being outside in the cold weather or from the long hours of standing.

Other children and families worked out in the fields when the weather was warmer. These people traveled from farm to farm, trying to survive. Children as young as three worked in any kind of weather doing hard physical labor. They picked cranberries, cotton, and sugar beets. Many worked fourteen hours a day until the picking was done.

Young laborers carry heavy loads of berries out of the fields.

One of the most dangerous places to work for children was in and around the dark, damp, and dusty coal mines. In mining, a breaker is a machine used to break rocks and coal. The youngest boys, often nine or ten years old, worked outside the mines as **breaker boys.** They sat on boards that hung over the coal chutes to work. They bent over and pulled out any slate or rock mixed in with the coal in the coal cars that sped by. It was dangerous work. These boys could reach down too far, fall, and be killed. The boys grew sick from bending over and breathing in coal dust all day long. Many developed chronic, or constant, coughs.

Breaker boys did back-breaking work, but they also had some power. Sometimes boys threw wood into the mining machinery, causing it to shut down for repairs so that they could have a little rest.

Life was just as hard for older boys who worked down in the mines. There was always the danger of explosions and cave-ins. These boys worked nine or ten hours, sometimes twelve hundred feet or more below the surface, in absolute darkness except for their small oil lamps. They were paid as little as eight cents an hour.

Young miners pose for a picture.

Winds of Change

At the turn of the twentieth century, more than two million children in the United States worked. They could not attend school, and few of them knew how to read or write.

Things were changing though. At one time child labor was seen as a fact of life, but reformers began to call attention to the problem. Lewis Hine gave a human face to child labor with his photos of working children. Mother Jones, Clara Lemlich, and other reformers organized marches and strikes to protest child labor.

In 1929 the stock market crashed. As a result many people lost their jobs, their savings, and their businesses. This was the beginning of the Great Depression, a worldwide drop in business that lasted from 1929 to the end of the 1930s. Slowly people began to change their minds about child labor being good for children, for industry, or for the family.

Mother Jones

A Missouri family sits on the edge of a highway after losing their home during the Great Depression.

During the Great Depression, about one fourth of the labor force was out of work. People began to rely on the government to help end the suffering. In 1938 the government decided that children under the age of sixteen could not work during school hours. It also decided that businesses could not give jobs to children instead of adults. These decisions were called the Fair Labor Standards Act.

Technology was changing too. Factories needed skilled workers to run and maintain the machines. Many jobs required more education, and states responded by increasing the number of years children were required to be in school.

In order to protect children, concerned citizens took responsibility to change child labor. The actions of these people, along with the effects of the Great Depression, brought positive reforms.

Time Line of Child Labor Reforms

1903

Labor organizer Mother Jones organizes a march of child textile workers and adult reformers from Philadelphia, Pennsylvania, to Long Island, New York.

1904

The National Child Labor Committee forms to publicize the truth about child labor.

1906

John Spargo writes a book telling how child textile workers breathe in dust from animal fur and skin as they make felt hats.

1908

Elizabeth Beardsley Butler reports on factory working conditions for girls, who work for even less pay than boys.

Photographer Lewis Hine takes pictures that shock citizens and help change public opinion.

1909

Clara Lemlich, a twenty-three-year-old garment worker, organizes a strike of more than twenty thousand garment workers.

1912
Florence Kelley fights to establish the United States Children's Bureau, a government group whose purpose is to improve the lives of children in society.

1913
The National Child Labor Committee writes the Declaration of Dependence.

1924
Congress passes an amendment to the Constitution to protect children under the age of eighteen in the workplace. But it fails to win approval of three-quarters of the states, and so does not become law.

1929
The stock market crashes, marking the beginning of the Great Depression.

1938
The Fair Labor Standards Act of 1938 helps promote child labor reform and prevents children from doing dangerous work.

Declaration of Dependence

By the Children of America in Mines
and Factories and Workshops Assembled

Whereas, We, Children of America, are declared to have been born free and equal, and

WHEREAS, We are yet in bondage in this land of the free; are forced to toil the long day or the long night, with no control over the conditions of labor, as to health or safety or hours or wages, and with no right to the rewards of our service, therefore be it

RESOLVED, I — That childhood is endowed with certain inherent and inalienable rights, among which are freedom from toil for daily bread; the right to play and to dream; the right to the normal sleep of the night season; the right to an education, that we may have equality of opportunity for developing all that there is in us of mind and heart.

RESOLVED, II — That we declare ourselves to be helpless and dependent that we are and of right ought to be dependent, and that we hereby present the appeal of our helplessness that we may be protected in the enjoyment of the rights of childhood.

RESOLVED, III — That we demand the restoration of our rights by the abolition of child labor in America.

National Child Labor Committee, 1913

Child Labor Today

All fifty U.S. states now have child labor laws to protect children in the workplace. Most states set a minimum wage, safety standards that include a required minimum age, and limits on the number of hours children under eighteen may work per week. However, labor laws have had little effect on the children of migrant farm workers who may number in the hundreds of thousands.

Tonight as you wash the dishes or feed your cat, think about your life and how different it might have been if you had lived one hundred years ago. Also, think about the people whose hard work to change child labor practices and laws made a difference for so many children. What could you do to make a difference in the world in your lifetime?

This worker meets her state's minimum age requirement to work.

Now Try This

Point of View

All people in history have a point of view. When studying any event in history, past or present, it is important to identify whose voices are heard and whose voices are silent. In this activity you will create the voice of one person's view about child labor. Share with partners who chose different points of view.

Who has a point of view about child labor?

1. ***Child's point of view.*** Think about working at one of the jobs mentioned in this book. Write a journal entry that describes one day in your life. What do you do and see? How do you feel? What do you think about while you work?

2. ***Employer's point of view.*** As the owner of a cotton mill, you depend on child labor. You believe strongly that children love to work and benefit from working. Write a paragraph questioning those who wish to reform child labor laws. Make your case in favor of it.

3. ***Parent's point of view.*** It is 1915. Even with everyone working, there is barely enough money to buy food. You want your children to have a happy life like the children you see playing in the park. Still, you desperately need the money your children can make, even though it is dangerous work that threatens their health and well-being. Make a chart that presents the pros and cons of sending your children off to work.

4. ***Your point of view.*** Lewis Hine's photographs capture the terrible truth about child labor in a way that words alone cannot do. Create a poster or drawings that express your ideas about children's rights as expressed in the Declaration of Dependence.

Glossary

bobbins *n.* reels or spools for holding thread, yarn, etc.

breaker boys *n.* workers who pull slate out of the coal cars in coal mines.

child labor *n.* using children under a certain age as workers in factories, businesses, etc.

dismay *n.* a sudden, helpless fear of what is about to happen or what has happened.

doffers *n.* workers who remove full bobbins and replace them with empty bobbins.

payroll *n.* list of persons to be paid and the amount that each one is to receive.

spinners *n.* workers who brush lint off the machines and watch for breaks in the thread in textile factories.

sweatshops *n.* places where workers are employed at low pay for long hours under bad conditions.

tenement houses *n.* buildings, especially in poor sections of the city, divided into sets of rooms occupied by separate families.

textile mills *n.* factories that make fabric.